MOODY MUSINGS

SURABHI DESAI

for You

Contents

Contents

Preface

for the mind that questions
and the heart that makes it understand.

1. LIFE

Life
Life is a mysterious lane
Without any doors or window pane
Yes we all think of it in different ways
because we all have individual timings
for unique sunsets to gaze
Sometimes we wish it wasn't a
mystery so we could have had a
better history
But what fun it would be to play a
game the outcome of which was
known to all
Where people would be wary of the
fall
Then there wouldn't be any lessons
to learn
nor would there be any
gratefulness for the outcome for
which we yearn.

2. CRAVE

What is it that with whole heart you
want
The thing without which life feels a
little gaunt
Is it a trip, a house, junk food or
health?
Or unlimited amount of wealth?
The heart craves for things it need
So pay the cravings a little heed
They might just carry an answer
To whether the craving is derived
from a feeling of lack or a feeling of greed.

3. HUNGER

Hunger is a word so small yet
so dark
With whom no one would wish to
cross path
Could be a feeling of emptiness and
pain
Which can be in reference to food
for the stomach or brain.
With it no one can thrive
however by being motivated by it
it gives you a yearning
for a successful life.

4. COLORS

The world is full of various colors
Some are dark
some are light
Some are chirpy
some are a like a neon vibe
Some are dark a tunnel
others as light as light.
But imagine if there was no
difference
Where all the colors existed with no
special feature
How would you express yourself in
any form of art?
The expression of sadness, jolly,
happy or pain?
The bliss of nature, the pearly drops
of rain
Would you ever want to put up such a
dull colorless art frame?

5. PERFECT

Perfection means to ace it all
To leave no room for improvement
and never fall
I don't know what it's like to be
perfect
But does it mean that is it any good?
Does being perfect in one thing
outshine being average at ten other things?
Genuinely how is a master of one
better than a jack of all trades?
Is the outstanding level based only
on perfect grades?
Because if that's the case then I don't
want to know how it feels
As I genuinely enjoy learning multiple
things which to my heart it sincerely
appeals.

6. ENVY

Time has passed long from the
Haves and the Have not
Yet why does it feel like not much has
changed?
We have food to eat
clothes to wear
A roof under which we sleep and have food
to share
But still we see empty eyes lurking
around
A feeling of sadness with no sound
The human evil form to go after what
the other has
Instead of appreciating the other truly
and living with class
It's a feeling that kills the person who
envies
And makes the other person thrive
more,
As it's the mindset of the person
which states
The other person has the best things
but the envious person shall always

have a soul that self stings.
And so shall it be till the person
realizes
That you have to be always happy for
others
For your sad envy hurts none but you
and you are the only one it bothers.

7. DESTINY

Some call it purpose
Some call it goal.
Whatever the meaning no one can
play foul.
It is described as a thing as written
in the stars
But reaching the destination might
lead to receive many scars.
Keep a track of your dreams don't let
them slip away
With hardwork and motivation you
shall reach your destined place
one day.

8. THINK

Think positive and positive takes
place
In the eye of the circumstances
maintain your grace
Like the tide won't stop for a little
breeze
Maintain your hope for the good
future with ease
We all face difficult things now and
then
But we should remember after the
scary storm falls the rain.

9. COLD

The day is colder than the nights
ever were,
The lights seem dimmer than the
dark in the far lane
The air seems to be dryer with a whiff of
pain,
But the meer thought of you makes
me want to dance in the rain
You seem farther than you ever were,
the memories of you seem blurr,
But just the glimpse of you makes me
feel warm than my sweater made of
furr.

10. PEOPLE PLEASER

She was a person who did as per her
will
But whenever she did so
they would talk of her ill
So she decided to live her life being
miss goody shoes
But such a decision led her life to be
full of blues.
What time she spent in pleasing all,
If only she could have used it to
prevent her big fall.

11. BLESSED

I am blessed beyond measure
I have food to eat, clothes to wear
and a place to call my own filled with
chores,
To eyes which can see everything
but I wish to see only the good,
To ears which are perfect for all the
good music which life can offer
Human is life's doll which gets to be
played with
filled with all kinds of things
twists and turns
But I know for sure everything comes
true for which my heart earnestly
yearns
I see my life filled with laughter and
blessings,
Some may say seeing life in rose
colored glasses is a waste of time
But then what's fun in always trying to
focus on the lemons
What is the use of sunshine and hay
when you choose to live in darkness

trying to make each color **gray**.

12. TREASURE

What is a treasure according to you?
Is it a chest full of riches or a genie in a
lamp to make your wishes come
true?
What if I told you the real treasure is
you being healthy all your life
To have your loved ones nearby
Would you be glad or would it feel
like a scam to you
That you merely get to exist and not
have a material wish granted for you?

13. SHARING

In school we were taught sharing,
To divide the things we have so it
seems like we are loving and caring.
But do you really believe that sharing is
caring?
What if one one day your morning is
filled with hunger
Would it remind you of the lessons
you were taught when you were
younger?

14. KIDS

The kids, they know how to be happy
To play, to live to act out their fantasy
But sadly it all comes to an end
When the height increases and so
does the list of our errands
But why should we live out a life of
glum and worry
To not stop for a breather and always
be in a hurry
We need to thrive and succeed
it's true
But shouldn't we learn to enjoy
and be calm or to enjoy the fresh
coffee brew?

15. SCHOOL DAYS

We grew up in a different day and
age
Where we were taught all different
stories of the sage
But now it's different with all the
awakening and rage
Which sometimes makes us feels we
were better in the safety cage
We just had to ace the exam and
attend school
Which when you think of it is pretty
cool
No tension, no worries, no choosing
the different life paths
Just drawing, languages and maths
we had to pass
As the days go by and each of us
survives
It was the time of least worries and
the best time of our lives.

16. FEELINGS

Feelings are as volatile as the time
They keep changing with every dime
Changing like the weather, season
and days
Sometimes they seem as jumbled as
a maze
But do pay attention your feelings
they are a big deal
They make you happy, glad and
joyful
making you live and helping
you heal
Like seasons they will change without
letting you know
But keep your head high focused on
the blessings and you shall forever
glow
When you focus on the good the
good shall have no other option buy
to grow.

17. WORRY

Worry is a thing that results in sweet
nothing
Like a rotten fruit it spreads its
condition
Nothing good comes from all the
tension
We strive to be happy and bubbly
But this tension just leaves me
feeling wobbly
Remember the many health
outcomes of this enemy
For it starts with the headache and
the lack of energy and nothing gets
better after it
Remember that thoughts are things
Who knows if with a little bit if hope
and manifestation what the future brings?

18. FAITH

Everyday can consist of many things
It depends on you whether you look
rusty or like diamond with bling
The biggest mindgames are
played by our own mind
Telling us we are either not worth it
or with ourselves we should not be kind
But there's another one which is quite
dangerous after all
It is a thinking that we are so gullible
or we have been so badly wronged
But wait a minute don't waste another
second trying to pity yourself
The higher power is watching and will
always care
Think of a worry and more worries
pile up
Pity yourself and you would find
yourself in the pits
Think clearly and keep a mind of your
own
Don't let anyone decide if you are
made up of grass or bone.

You will always lose trying to fight
with a clown
because he is the star
of the circus so you should know
Like attracts like so be different than
the rest
Put faith in the universe and level up
to be the best.

19. QUIET

I love the way how the quiet speaks
Of thoughts and cricket noise it
reeks
Life gets lost on all the attempts to fill
the pages
Hence it feels like solitude was last
experienced before ages
Too much of nothing leads to any
good
Being alone and lonely do
not belong under the same hood
As being alone is spending time by
yourself
and being lonely feels like in
a world so vaste you are a sad elf.

20. MAIN CHARACTER

How I wish to see if people played
the main
In this story of life with a very clear
aim
But not many can be what they call
main character
As people are more curious about the
other person's banter
The more you see, talk and think
about the other person's activity
Will amount to form in your life the
same size of huge cavity
Imagine if you use the time you
spend thinking about other people's
business on yourself
You would reach your goal so much
quicker even if it were put on the
highest shelf.

21. PREDICT

How great would it be to figure out
life's timing
Where we wouldn't wonder whether
we would ever receive what we wish
for
Or live a life with empty wishes
galore
But oh what fun would it be
with no suspense or imagining a fantasy
to live a live already predicted
with no surprise or any feeling of ectasy.

22. MISSING YOU

We all have a person we miss alot
Talking about whom we get caught
Who was gone too soon but I guess
the time was right
With whom we fought alot but still
were friends with by night
The person who we were so used to
talking to and have fond memories
with
Who was an example that selflessly
caring for a person is not a myth
To my person I say I wasn't able to
thank you for all the things
As the mere thought of you, all the
childhood memories it brings
One day in the future we shall meet
again
Where I will again teach you to read and
write in English with a paper and pen.

23. LAUGH

Laugh a little
Laugh alot
Laugh with no sound, hysterically or
a snort
Life is too short to spend it being
glum
Maybe try laughing as who doesn't
want cheeks which look like plum?
Nobody likes to look at a face which
looks grumpy
Why not laugh a little everyday
Who knows, maybe being happy
might keep the gloomy days away.

24. WORTH

When you ask for something to be
yours in this life
Do you actually believe you are worth
it?
Do you just wish for it and don't strive
for it in your life
But pretend you have done enough
with white lies
If you couldn't fool yourself to believe,
do you think without even a little bit of
effort and work you would be entitled
to aim and achieve?

25. TIME

Time is funny or a weird fragment
whatever you may assume
It's limited of ofcourse like the spray
of a perfume
One moment you can feel it and in
the other its gone
You would have either used it to
snooze around
or like a diamond you
might have shone
But the sad thing about time is you
don't take it seriously till it's gone
Maybe next time live in the moment
rather than the past or in future form.

26. DIFFERENT

Like a chip in a packet,
Like the different colored eye sockets
Like the various handerkerchiefs in
different pockets
Dare to be different and exist like you
If you live to observe and pick
ideas from others as yours to reserve,
You will be just letting go of what you
actually deserve
Because darling in life only the
originals have a good life and price
the seconds and the thirds are
as good as sewer's mice.

27. RAIN

First its sunny
then gloomy it gets
Before you know it the sun has set
Then it becomes dark and the trees
start to sway
You look out from the windows at the
windy roads in dismay
The weather forecast is easy to
estimate
But you know the cozy weather will
make you procrastinate
And suddenly it starts raining heavily
again
So you just sit with a coffee and
book on your bed
Somedays it's good to sit back and
chill
Taking in the scenic views or go for a
car ride in the hills
For life is all about the unpredictable
events
So why not just relax someday and
take in all the wet soil scents.

28. LOST

Sometimes the feeling of dark takes
over
Where it feels like there is any empty
feeling in the soul
A feeling of lack, a depth or a huge
hole.
It takes over when there are many
questions in mind
Asking me why am I not taking part in
the grind.
At such a time I let my mind be at
rest
Reminding it that this is just a test,
Take a breath and be at ease
There is no one in th world other than
ourself to please
So no matter what questions the
mind decides to throw your way
Just try to give your best in anything
you do, work hard and let destiny do
its part in the play.

29. COFFEE

Chai, coffee ,matcha or juice each to
its own
It's not the name but the power it
holds
Waking up and having it has become
a habit
Like a carrot chasing cute rabbit,
First thing in the morning or several
cups in the day
Loving it so much that to think it has
the power to make hay
Bad vibes, sadness is what it keeps
at bay
But darling remember you deserve
some credit too
do give your soul some applause
for not letting you hang your head down
in dismay.

30. GIVE THANKS

No matter what life gives you
Whether sadness or happiness or a
mixture of the two
Don't ever let a day go by without
giving thanks
It's only the grateful hearts which are
always at the higher ranks.
Happiness, joy, sadness
ups and downs
are part of our life to make us feel alive
Let us not forget that even the
darkest days have a limited time in
our life to stay.

Thank You

You have made it to the end. Thankyou for giving your time and patience and reading it till the end. I hope you have seen a part of my musings and been able to feel the meanings of my thoughts and ramblings. I hope your eyes saw only goodness and any fault if existed was overlooked. A sense of connection and similarity was what this book was intended to create. I would say it was a success if you felt it even for a fleeting second. Sending lots of love and happiness your way. May we always believe in miracles and reap the benefits of everything good the universe has to offer.

-a letter from me to You

www.ingramcontent.com/pod-product-compliance
Lightning Source LLC
Chambersburg PA
CBHW020517160726
47991CB00007B/3000